POSTMODERN ALCHEMISTS

The Architecture of Desire and the Economy of Illusion

Bookarion

POSTMODERN ALCHEMISTS

The Architecture of Desire and the Economy of Illusion

Ekrem KÜÇÜK

ISBN: 978-625-5765-29-1
e-ISBN: 978-625-5765-30-7

June 2026

Editor
Tuğba ATAMTÜRK

Publishing Coordinator
Dr. Dilek KURBAN

Academic Consultant
Assoc. Prof. Dr. Elvan ATAMTÜRK

Cover, Interior Design & E-Book
Bookarion Visual Arts

Offset Printing
Murat Can Açan - Punto Ajans | Certificate No: 44527
Seyrantepe Mh. İbrahim Karaoğlanoğlu Cd. No:105/124 Kâğıthane/İstanbul

Bookarion

Seyrantepe Mah. Gökdeniz Sok. No:15/3
34413 – Kâğıthane – İstanbul – Türkiye
www.bookarion.com info@bookarion.com

bookarion bookarion bookarion bookarion bookarion
bookarion bookarion bookarion bookarion bookarion

Bookarion® *and* **Bookarion Scholar®** *are publishing imprints of Smart and Start Intelligent Financial Solutions Consulting and Publishing Inc...*

POSTMODERN ALCHEMISTS

The Architecture of Desire and the Economy of Illusion

EKREM KÜÇÜK

Bookarion

"Et eunt homines mirari alta montium et ingentes fluctus maris et latissimos lapsus fluminum et oceani ambitum et gyros siderum, et relinquunt se ipsos."

"And people admire the heights of the mountains, the giant waves of the sea, the broad beds of the rivers, the vastness of the ocean, and even the orbits of the stars, yet they neglect themselves..."

— **Saint Augustine,** ***Confessions***

To my mother, my guide,

to my wife, my companion,

and to my daughter, my light...

PREFACE

When you flip through history books, you notice a strange cycle. Clothes change, technologies change, currencies change, but one figure never changes: The Alchemist. Sometimes they appear in a medieval king's court, holding a flask full of mercury. Sometimes they emerge in 1920s Boston, holding postal coupons. Sometimes they show up on Wall Street in the 2020s, with complex charts on a screen behind them, and sometimes on Instagram in front of a rented Ferrari. Their names, languages, and methods are all different, but the product they sell is one and the same: The Shortcut.

We modern humans think we are smarter than the people of the past. We say, "Medieval people were ignorant and superstitious, that's why they fell for alchemists.". Yet in the 21st century, while carrying phones in our pockets that can access all the libraries in the world; we still hope to "get rich overnight," "lose weight with a single pill," or "find love by sending messages to the universe." Why?

Because no matter how much technology advances, the Human Operating System (Human OS) hasn't received an update in the last 200,000 years. We are still greedy. We are still afraid. We still hate uncertainty. And most importantly; we are still looking for the "Philosopher's Stone," that magic wand that will effortlessly turn life's hardships into gold.

Alchemists don't die because this "hunger" inside us doesn't die. They are not merely scammers; they are the most skilled hackers of human nature. They know our weaknesses, desires, and fears better than we do.

This book is not an exposé. This book is not a "History of Alchemy" either. This book is the courage to look in the mirror. While reading how Newton was fooled, why people went crazy during the Tulip Mania, or how Anna Delvey wrapped everyone around her little finger, you will actually see yourself there. If we want to survive the Alchemists' laboratory, we must first understand how they work. If you are ready, we are slightly opening the door to that laboratory.

CONTENTS

PREFACE i

INTRODUCTION 1

The Dark Vaults of Hamburg and the First Big Lie 1

What is Alchemy, Who is an Alchemist? 5

Fighting with Time: Mircea Eliade's Observation 5

The Alchemist's Formula 6

Augustine 2.0: Digital Confessions 7

Entering the Laboratory 8

CHAPTER 1
EXILED FROM EDEN "HOMO ECONOMICUS" 9

The Perfect Market Hypothesis and "Boring" Abundance..... 9

The Whisper Network and the First "Insider" Information 14

The Moment of Decision:
The Second the Brain Glitched 15

And the Bubble Bursts: The Great Disappointment 16

Blue Eggs and the Unbearable Weight of the "Quince" (Screwing Up) 18

The "Effortless Village" Simulation 19

And the Great Awakening: Apple or Quince?....................20
Free Cheese is Only Found in a Mousetrap.............................. 21
The Original Sin of Economics: The Desire for Costless Gain 21
Homo Economicus is Dead, Long Live "Bounded Rationality"!..22
Conclusion: Entering the Laboratory.................................... 23

CHAPTER 2 THE GLOW IN THE DARK AND THE FIRST "PUFFERS" 25

Isaac Newton's Secret Chest and the Bankruptcy of Reason25
Why Do the Smartest Also Fall For It?.................................... 26
Entering the Alchemy Laboratory..28
The Alchemist's Trick Box: Virus Updated 29
Modern Times: The "F12" Key Replaced the Wand 30
The Second Rule of the Alchemist: The Illusion of Complexity 31
Gravity Is Unforgiving: The Bankruptcy of a Genius and the Gallows 32
Newton's "Apocalypse" in the Stock Market.......................... 32
The End of Charlatans: Gold-Plated Gallows 34
Conclusion: You Reap What You Sow...................................... 35

CHAPTER 3 FLOWERS, CHAINS, AND THE GREATER FOOL THEORY 37

History's Most Expensive Bulb and Waiting for the Greater Fool 37

The Million-Dollar Breakfast 38
The Greater Fool Theory 39
The Alchemist's New Laboratory: The Stock Market 40
When the Music Stops: Nigredo and the Sound of Silence .. 41
Alchemy Backfires: Turning from Gold to Lead 42
Lesson: Being Able to Say "The Emperor Has No Clothes" ... 43
Mr. Alchemist Takes the Stage: Charles Ponzi 44
How the "System" Worked? (Or Didn't Work) 45
Paying the Old Investor with the New 46
The Collapse and Modern Heirs 46
Today's Ponzis: The Name Changed, The Logic is the Same 47
Conclusion: The Mathematics of Greed 47

CHAPTER 4
THE ALCHEMIST'S MIRROR AND THE ART OF PRETENDING 49

New York's Fake Princess: Anna Delvey's Magic Mirror 49
- The Power of Non-Existent Money 50
- Social Arbitrage: Turning Nothingness into Status 51

Rented Ferraris and Digital Narcotics 52
- Private Jet Studios and Hourly Wealth 52
- The Alchemy of Filters: Lead Faces, Golden Visages 53
- Digital Narcotics: The Dopamine Cycle 54

Alchemy in the Ballot Box: Post-Truth and the Allure of the Lie 55
- "Truth" is Now a Boring Detail! 55

The Alchemy of Nostalgia: The Lie of the "Good Old Days" 56
Why Do Lies Spread at the Speed of Light? 57
Conclusion: The Face in the Mirror 58

CHAPTER 5
THE BAZAAR OF THE SOUL AND MODERN SHAMANS 59

Marrying Quantum and Spiritual Materialism 59
"I Am Enlightened, It's Your Turn (VAT Included)" 60
Word Games: The Quantum Refuge 61
Santiago's Treasure and the Wrong Map 62
The Universe Is Not an Order Hotline! 63
The Title Deed to Heaven and the "Fireproof Shroud" Market 64
The Alchemist's Greatest Trump Card: Guaranteed Salvation 65
Transfer of Will: "Escape from Freedom" 65
"The Chosen One" Marketing 66
Conclusion: Alchemy Backfires 67
The Lonely Hearts Club and Placebo Priests 67
Love Bombing 68
Placebo Priests: Dumbo's Feather 69
The Sunk Cost Fallacy: Why Can't We Wake Up? 70
Conclusion: The Alchemist is Within Us 71

CONCLUSION
THE SONG OF THE SIRENS AND TYING ONESELF TO THE MAST 73
The Masts of the Modern World: Pre-commitment 74
True Alchemy: The Triumph of the Boring 76
Final Word: The Captain's Cabin 77

CONCEPT INVENTORY 79
INTRODUCTION & CHAPTER 79
Alchemy 79
Philosopher's Stone (Lapis Philosophorum) 79
Use Value vs. Exchange Value 79
CHAPTER 2 80
Intelligence Paradox (The Intelligence Trap) 80
Puffers 80
Illusion of Complexity (Complexity Bias) 80
CHAPTER 3 80
The Greater Fool Theory 80
FOMO (Fear of Missing Out) 81
Nigredo (Black Phase) 81
CHAPTER 4 81
Post-Truth 81
Fake It Till You Make It 81
Snapchat Dysmorphia 81
Simulacra 82
CHAPTER 5 82
Spiritual Materialism 82
Placebo Effect 82

Sunk Cost Fallacy 82
Love Bombing 82
CONCLUSION 83
Pre-commitment 83
Ulysses Contract 83

BIBLIOGRAPHY AND INSPIRING WORKS 85
Books 85
Articles and Research 87

Bookarion

INTRODUCTION

The Dark Vaults of Hamburg and the First Big Lie

Hamburg, 1669.

A bankrupt merchant named Hennig Brand had been battling an unbearable stench in his basement for days, even weeks. His neighbors thought he had gone mad, and they weren't entirely wrong, because Brand had accumulated exactly 5,000 liters of human urine in his basement. Yes, you heard that right. Urine. Brand was neither a pervert nor a hygiene-obsessed cleaner; he was the most passionate "alchemist" of his time.

His theory, viewed with today's rational mind, was comical, but in the mystical world of that era, it was highly logical: Gold was yellow, and human urine was also yellow. If he boiled the urine at the right temperature, distilled it, and combined it with the right chemicals, he could reveal nature's hidden essence and turn that yellow liquid into pure gold. For days he waited by the alembics amidst that terrible smell, until finally, he saw a glimmer at the bottom of the boiling liquid. A whitish substance glowing in the dark, burning like a candle. Brand's heart began to beat out of his chest. He was certain he had found that legendary "Philosopher's Stone" sought for centuries. Now he was rich, he was immortal, he was no longer a "nobody" but a "chosen one.".

However, what he found wasn't gold. It was phosphorus. Hennig Brand went down in history by boiling thousands of liters of urine for the sake of getting rich, but he never achieved the fortune he expected. His story is the most tragicomic summary of human history:

> *Wasting the reality you have (time, effort, and dignity) in pursuit of a non-existent treasure.*

Today, we laugh at Brand's state in that basement and say, "How stupid he was." But is it really so? Scroll up your screen. That flutter you feel when you see a "finance guru" on Instagram saying "Earn dollars while you sleep"... That "fear of missing out" (FOMO) in your stomach when you see a coin you've never even heard of surge 3000% in 24 hours on a crypto exchange... Or that secret hope when you click on an ad claiming "This cream will make you

20 years younger"... How are these any different from the hope Hennig Brand felt looking at his cauldron full of urine? There is no difference. The mechanism is the same; only the decor has changed. Today, Brand's alembics have been replaced by stock market charts, alchemy formulas by complex algorithms, and the Philosopher's Stone by promises of "financial freedom.".

The human brain, that 1.5-kilogram jelly-like organ inside our skulls, has barely changed in the last 50,000 years. We are still using that old hardware that tries to survive in the savanna, is programmed to save energy (i.e., laziness), and is scared to death of uncertainty. When this hardware sees an "effortless and huge reward," the prefrontal cortex—the logic center of our brain—flips the switch. All that's left are impulses, desires, and that ancient hunger.

This book is not a history of fraud. This book is not a financial literacy lesson either. This book is the story of why we want to be fooled.

Whatever motivation led Adam and Eve to that forbidden tree was the same motivation that made people believe they could turn lead into gold in the 17th century. And today, in the plazas of the 21st century, on smartphone screens and in election squares, the motivation pushing us into the lap of the "Postmodern Alchemists" is still the same.

When the Devil handed Adam the apple, he didn't say, "Here, this is very tasty.". As stated in the Quran, he said, *"Shall I show you the tree of immortality and a kingdom that will never decay?"* (Surah Taha, verse 120). What was promised was not an apple; what was promised was a godliness obtained through a shortcut, it was immortality, it was effortless power.

Alchemy is the oldest and most stubborn disease in human history: The desire to bypass the laws of nature, skip the process, and reach the result (the reward) by cheating. Throughout history, these alchemists disguised themselves; sometimes they appeared as robed sorcerers, sometimes as suited bankers, and sometimes as influencers sharing filtered photos. But the product they sold was always the same: *Hope.* And we were always more than ready to buy that hope.

If you are ready, we are entering the laboratory. But this time, there is no urine or mercury in the test tube. This time, our own minds are under the lens.

Welcome...

What is Alchemy, Who is an Alchemist?

What Hennig Brand did in that dark basement might seem like madness. But his goal was to realize the greatest dream of human history: Turning the worthless (lead/urine) into the valuable (gold). In its classical definition, Alchemy is the ancestor of chemistry; it is the art of transmuting metals and finding the elixir of immortality.

However, the "Postmodern Alchemy" we will discuss in this book is about perceptions, not elements. According to our definition, an Alchemist is a person who transforms something that doesn't actually exist or has very little value (a dream, a crypto token, a lifestyle, or a political promise) into a "Priceless" treasure in the eyes of people.

Fighting with Time: Mircea Eliade's Observation

Seeing alchemy merely as "greed for gold" is incomplete; a much deeper desire lies at its philosophical root. Mircea Eliade, an expert in the history of religions and mythology, defines this desire in his masterpiece "The Forge and the Crucible" as: "Accelerating Time.". According to Eliade, ancient people believed that ores "grew" underground and turned into gold after a natural maturation process lasting thousands of years. The alchemist, using the fire in his laboratory, claimed: "What nature does in thousands of years, I can do in a few weeks by accelerating it in my crucible.". Thus, the Alchemist was the one who challenged the rhythm of nature and time, assuming a Divine power by shortening the processes.

This is where our roots merge with Postmodern Alchemists. Today's alchemist is also at odds with "Time.".

- They say, "You don't need to work 40 years to get rich" (Accelerates time).
- They say, "You don't need to wait for the relationship to mature, apply this tactic" (Shortens the process).
- They say, "You don't need to read books to be informed, watch this 10-minute video" (Eliminates effort).

As Eliade said, the Alchemist promises to "eliminate Time," and since impatience is the modern human's greatest disease, this promise always finds a buyer.

The Alchemist's Formula

An alchemist is not a magician; he is an "Arbitrage Master.". Arbitrage of what?. The difference between Reality and Expectation. Life is hard, boring, and slow (Reality). People want life to be easy, exciting, and fast (Expectation). The Alchemist builds a bridge between these two points.

- Working is hard -> The Alchemist sells "Passive Income".
- Facing oneself is hard -> The Alchemist sells "Filters".
- Uncertainty is scary -> The Alchemist sells "Guarantees".

The Alchemist does not sell you a "product." He sells you a "story," and the human brain is coded in a way that it cannot resist a well-told story.

Augustine 2.0: Digital Confessions

You read Saint Augustine's striking words spoken centuries ago at the opening of the book. He complained about people being mesmerized by the splendor of nature while neglecting their own souls. If Augustine lived today and walked the streets, plazas, or cafes of the modern city with a smartphone in hand, he would probably update his Confessions as follows:

"And modern humans admire the dizzying heights of crypto charts and stock candles, the giant waves of likes and interactions, the deceptive vastness of limitless 'choices' and virtual promises, and the flawless orbits of the dream of 'being someone else,' yet they neglect their own potentials, their own efforts, and their own realities...".

The difference is this: In the past, what blinded humans to themselves was the immense greatness of nature. Today, what blinds us to ourselves are the artificial glitters created by Alchemists. We have turned into a generation that cannot find the time to live our own lives because we are busy watching the lives others "Pretend to Have". Our eyes are always outside, always on someone else's display window, and that is exactly what the Alchemists want:

Keep your eyes glued to that window so you don't notice what's going on in the back (the kitchen) of the shop.

Now is the time to break the glass of that display window and enter the kitchen in the back.

Entering the Laboratory

In this book, we will visit the masters who set up their laboratories in different periods of history. Sometimes in a stock exchange building, sometimes in a palace, and sometimes on an Instagram profile.... You will see that; Although the materials change (sometimes a tulip bulb, sometimes a postal coupon, sometimes a digital coin), the formula is always the same: Fuel the desire, disable the mind, and sell the dream.

Now, let's go to the Garden of Eden, where history's first and biggest sale was made. Because the first Alchemist was waiting for his customer there, on the branch of a tree.

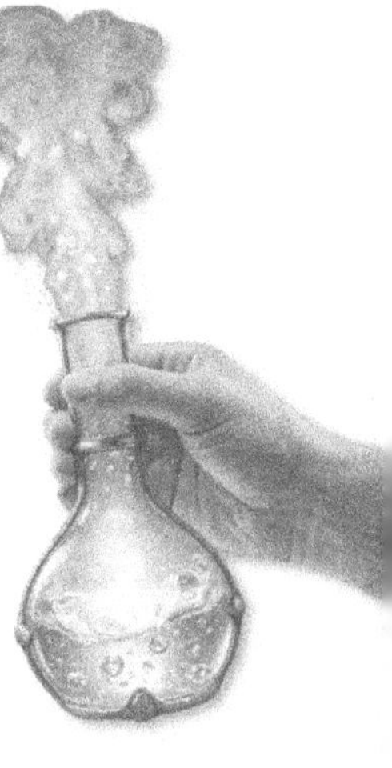

CHAPTER 1
EXILED FROM EDEN
"HOMO ECONOMICUS"

The Perfect Market Hypothesis and "Boring" Abundance

Economics defines itself with a single word in the very first lesson taught to students in the cold lecture halls of universities: Scarcity. Textbooks start by saying, "Human needs are unlimited, but resources are limited.". All stock market charts, interest rate decisions, wars, and trade agreements are built upon this simple truth. If there were enough of everything for everyone, there would be no such thing as price. Where there is no price, there is no trade; where there is no trade, there is no money; and where there is no money, there are no banks. So, economics is actually the science of the "Expulsion from Eden.".

However, we must return to the beginning of the story, right before that moment of expulsion. Because that strange software of the human mind, prone to being scammed, deceived, and "desiring what doesn't exist," was coded not in a world of scarcity, but in Eden, where there was abundance.

Imagine the first and only known "Perfect Market" in history. Whether it was in the plains of Mesopotamia or in another dimension beyond time and space, let's leave that to the theologians. Let's look at that environment through the lens of a behavioral economist: It was a utopian economic model that adorns the dreams of every modern consumer and every Wall Street investor. Here, the marginal cost was zero. You didn't need to take out your wallet, consider your credit card limit, or wait for the end of the month for a fruit you reached out and picked when you were hungry. There was no housing problem; there was no issue of rent increase rates, real estate bubbles, or tensions with landlords. Most importantly, there was no future anxiety; questions like "What will I eat tomorrow?", "What will I do when I retire?", or "What if I get sick?" did not exist in the vocabulary of that market.

Adam and Eve were the first residents of this Economic Nirvana; they were literally the "Children of the System.". Every need they had was met before that need even appeared in their minds; the time between desire and satisfaction was zero seconds.

So, what can you sell to a human living in such an environment?. This is the most terrifying nightmare for a marketer: A customer who has everything. Where there is no need, there is no demand. Where there is no demand, there are no sales. And where there are no sales, manipulation seems impossible.

However, deep within human nature (fitrah), there is a much darker and insatiable hunger that has nothing to do with stomach hunger or the need for shelter. A piece of data that economists cannot calculate and that does not reflect on the charts of statistical institutes. This data is "Ontological Insecurity.". That is, the doubt of: "I exist, I am here, I have everything but... What if all this ends one day? What if I am not actually as special as I think I am?".

Right at this point, the first "Alchemist" of history steps onto the stage. He has no tangible product to sell; not a car, not a house, not a treasury bond. He only has a "story.". As the Devil watched Adam and Eve, he focused not on what they had, but on the single thing they didn't have. Amidst that immense abundance, in that perfect "all-inclusive" resort, only one thing was missing: The authority to cross boundaries. Humans, by nature, were limited beings; limited by space, limited by time, and limited by that one single prohibition (that notorious tree) set by the Creator. That single "No!" within perfection turned into a maggot growing over time in Adam's mind.

In the modern world, we call this "Opportunity Cost.". Adam could eat all the fruits in Eden; billions of options. But his mind was on that single one he couldn't eat, because prohibition is the most potent aphrodisiac of desire. The Alchemist (Devil) built his marketing strategy entirely on this "Forbidden = Valuable" equation. He didn't go to Adam and say, "Are you hungry?" (because he knew he wasn't). He didn't say, "Do you want a more luxurious house?" (because he was in the most beautiful garden). He asked him the exact same question that crypto scammers, Ponzi scheme leaders, or heavily-makeupped Instagram influencers ask today:

"What you have is beautiful, Adam. But what if there is more? What if you are actually more than just a human? Do you want me to whisper to you that secret formula that will carry you beyond these boundaries, that will 'Angelicize' you (take you to a divine dimension)?".

This was the first "Leverage" offer in history. The Devil was offering Adam to gain an imaginary asset (Immortality/Godliness) by risking his existing asset (peace in Eden). What should Adam, as a rational "Homo Economicus", have done?. He should have done a risk analysis.

- **Existing asset:** Infinite comfort, zero risk, 100% guarantee.

- **Promised asset:** Becoming an angel, infinite power. (Probability of happening: Uncertain, Source: An unreliable stranger).

Mathematically, he should have rejected this offer. No sane investor would burn their guaranteed treasure for some obscure tip. But Adam burned it.... Eve burned it.... And we, as their children, have continued to make the same mistake with the same excitement for thousands of years. Why?. Because the Alchemist does not sell us a product. The Alchemist sells us the dream of our own potential. When Adam reached for that tree, he thought he was buying not the fruit, but the "Super-Adam" he would transform into when he ate that fruit. Just like today, a civil servant who enters a Ponzi scheme promising 50% monthly profit thinks they are buying not the money, but the "free, resignation-handing-to-the-boss, vacationing-in-Dubai Super-Self" they will get with that money.

In this first session, we understand this: The problem was not the fruit (the product). The problem was not even the Devil (the seller). The problem was the unfillable void inside Adam (the consumer). The desire for "more".... Economic historians usually describe the Tulip Mania as the first bubble. However, the first bubble was inflated in Eden. And when that bubble burst, it wasn't just wallets that went bankrupt, but human destiny as well.

The Whisper Network and the First "Insider" Information

It was one of those calm, windless, and overly perfect afternoons in Eden. Adam was probably experiencing that slight metal fatigue (boredom) brought by the eternity he possessed under the shade of the trees. Right at that moment, the villain of our story entered the stage. But not as a monster holding a spear and breathing fire from its mouth as you might expect. He was disguised as history's first "Life Coach.". Perhaps he came in the form of a friend, or perhaps just as a soft tone of voice carried by the wind. And he dropped the magic question, which is the most fundamental rule of modern marketing today, onto Adam's shoulder:

"Why?".

"Why is everything in this garden yours, but that tree in the middle is forbidden? Don't you think there are things not being told to you here?".

This question was the first conspiracy theory seed dropped into Adam's mind. The Alchemist (Devil) had set up his strategy perfectly. He did not praise the product (the forbidden fruit). First, he created a Trust Deficit against the existing authority (the Creator/System). Whatever emotion you feel today when you see the title "The secret banks are hiding from you!" on a YouTube video, that was exactly what Adam felt at that moment: "Something is being kept from me.".

And the Alchemist continued his whisper. With a fairy-tale promise, he presented the first "Insider Trading" offer in history: "Look Adam, the reason it's forbidden to you is not that the fruit is poisonous. On the contrary... That fruit carries the source codes of the system. If you take a bite of it, you will no longer be the ruled, but the ruler. You will become the eternal owner of the property, not a mortal tenant. You will become angelic. That means... You will attain divine power.".

Look at the immensity of the offer. What was on the table was not a simple apple (or wheat). What was on the table was a leap in status. The Alchemist was telling Adam: "You are currently a beta version human. This fruit is your key to transition to the pro version, to premium membership. Why settle for the standard package?".

The Moment of Decision: The Second the Brain Glitched

As Adam walked towards that tree, he was actually becoming the guinea pig of the first Behavioral Economics Experiment. Under normal conditions, the rational mind (Frontal Cortex) should have stepped in and said: "Wait a minute! Who is making me this offer? What is his reference? Who has he turned into an angel before? Plus, is it worth taking this risk? I already have eternal life, why risk the prohibition and lose everything?".

But at that moment, a very dangerous mechanism kicked in inside Adam's brain (and today in ours): Hyperbolic Discounting. The human brain perceives a tangible pleasure it will get now as much more valuable than a probable punishment it will face in the future. The Alchemist brought the fruit (the reward) right in front of Adam's eyes, right to the tip of his nose. The smell, the shine, the promise of the fruit was so close that; the risk of future expulsion blurred, faded, and turned into an insignificant detail in Adam's mind.

When dopamine (the desire hormone) starts to be secreted, logic leaves the building. When Adam bit into that fruit, he hadn't even tasted it yet. What intoxicated him was not the taste of the fruit, but the dream of what the fruit would bring him. This is the Alchemists' greatest secret: They never sell the product. They sell the transformation the product will make you feel. The alchemist selling makeup does not sell paint; they sell beauty and being admired. The stock market speculator does not sell shares; they sell financial freedom. The Devil does not sell fruit; he sells eternity.

And the Bubble Bursts: The Great Disappointment

Adam and Eve took only a single bite to wake up from that magical moment, from that fairy-tale dream of ascension. As soon as their teeth sank into the fruit, those golden-glowing lights, angel wings, or divine power promised by the Alchemist did not arrive. The exact opposite happened. Suddenly, that spiritual armor, that veil of innocence over them, was lifted. Alchemy had backfired. While expecting to become angels, they were left naked. While expecting to become eternal property owners, they were left homeless (exiled from Eden).

This was the first "Rug Pull" operation in history. The Alchemist (Devil) gathered liquidity with his promise, drove excitement to its peak, and pulled the plug right at the moment of the transaction. Adam was left standing there with half an apple and great shame. The Alchemist had already retreated to his corner to wait for the next victim (namely, Adam's descendants). Because after that day, the following was written into humanity's genetic code: "The forbidden is attractive. The shortcut must always be tried. And when someone tells you 'You are very special,' they should be believed.".

Here is our story, built upon this genetic legacy. That desire for momentary enrichment/empowerment that Adam felt under that tree that day continues to beat in exactly the same way in the heart of everyone who invests in Çiftlik Bank, opens a crypto leveraged trade, or kisses the hem of fake sheikhs today. The venue changed. The fruit changed. But the bite is the same bite.

Blue Eggs and the Unbearable Weight of the "Quince" (Screwing Up)

Now let's move the camera from under that tree in Mesopotamia thousands of years forward, to the Turkey of 2016, among the plazas and shopping malls. History books tell us events in a chronological order: The Stone Age, the Iron Age, the Industrial Revolution, the Information Age... As if humanity is on a constantly progressing, developing, and getting-smarter timeline. This is a massive lie. Although the technical history of humanity changes, its psychological history is cyclical. Decors, costumes, and accessories change, but the script never changes. Whatever the operating system of the first human Adam was, the operating system of the modern human looking at their latest model smartphone today is exactly the same (except for a few minor updates).

Therefore, the emergence in 2016 of a sympathetic but sketchy youth in his 20s nicknamed "Tosuncuk" (The Chubby, a scammer, a notorious Turkish Ponzi scheme leader) who defrauded thousands of people is not a judicial case; it is an evolutionary repetition. Tosuncuk, namely Mehmet Aydın, was the alchemist of modern times. He had very well analyzed the offer the Devil presented to Adam. What was Adam's problem? "Being limited." Getting tired, getting hungry, having to wait. Tosuncuk offered to sell people back exactly what Adam lost, the "Virtual Eden.".

The "Effortless Village" Simulation

The "Çiftlik Bank" (Farm Bank) that Tosuncuk established was not a simple Ponzi scheme. It was a psychological masterpiece. He told people: "Raising cows in the real world is hard. The barn smells, the animal gets sick, feed is expensive, milk doesn't make money. Come and buy my chickens that lay blue eggs, my virtual cows. No sweating. No risk. No waiting. Just sit at the computer, let your cows work for you, and you just collect the profit like a divine overseer.".

This sentence is the digital translation of the sentence the Devil whispered to Adam, "Eat from the tree of immortality, never die.". Normally, a sane doctor, engineer, or teacher should biologically and mathematically know that a cow cannot amortize itself in 3 months. But knowing is not enough. Because the mechanism we are facing works on impulse, not knowledge.

The Alchemist does not make his victim feel like a fool. On the contrary, he makes them feel like the "Genius Who Found the Glitch in the System.". Those who invested in Çiftlik Bank looked down with pity on other people who got up in the morning to go to work and worked for a salary. Just like Adam thinking he would be superior to other creatures when he ate the fruit. People did not fall in love with Tosuncuk's lie; they fell in love with that desire for effortless mercy within themselves.

And the Great Awakening: Apple or Quince?

There is no difference in terms of method between the Devil promising Adam eternity and throwing him into the mortal world; and Tosuncuk promising high profits and fleeing to Uruguay. In both, the bubble bursts. In both, that sweet dream gives way to an ice-cold reality. When Adam bit the forbidden fruit, he was expecting that unique flavor on his palate. The Çiftlik Bank victim, on the other hand, was expecting millions to be deposited into their account.

But history is nothing but repetition. In the end; when it was understood that what was eaten was not an apple but a quince (trouble), it was already too late for everything. This is fitrah (human nature)... Even though humanity has carried that bitter experience in its genes for thousands of years, every time it cannot help but surrender to the allure of that apple (or virtual cow, or cryptocurrency). Because "eating the quince" (screwing up) is in our factory settings. We are programmed to fall. Because we cannot stop without falling (making mistakes), without tasting that forbidden fruit, without pushing the limits.

Therefore, do not look at those thousands of people who were victims of Çiftlik Bank and say "How stupid they are!". They were simply loyal children properly bearing the legacy of their father Adam. They fell victim to the desire to "return to Eden" within themselves. Tosuncuk was just an intermediary. The real culprit was the lazy and greedy circuits of our brain looking for that shortcut. And rest assured; tomorrow when someone else comes out holding a new apple that looks shinier, more technological, and more guaranteed... We will get in line again. We will say, "This time is different". We will say, "This time the apple is sweet". And we will probably eat the quince again.

Free Cheese is Only Found in a Mousetrap

As we close this first part of our story, we need to take an x-ray of that thousands-of-years-long adventure of "Eating the Quince" stretching from Adam to Tosuncuk. Because this book is not a "history of fraud" book. This book is not a financial literacy guide either. This book is an analysis of that futile war human engages in with their own nature (fitrah) and loses every single time.

So, what is the name of this war?. Economists call it "Opportunity Cost." Physicists call it the "Laws of Thermodynamics." The wisdom of Anatolia says, "You reap what you sow.". They all lead to the same door: There is nothing for nothing in the universe.

The Original Sin of Economics: The Desire for Costless Gain

Let's remember what the invoice for being expelled from Eden was: "By the sweat of your brow you will eat your food.". This sentence is the greatest trauma in human history. Because from that moment on, human was exiled from a "Zero Cost" (Eden) world to a "Cost > 0" (World) system. Now wheat is needed for bread, a field for wheat, water for the field, and labor for water. There is no output without input. No work can be done without expending energy.

The very reason for the existence of Alchemists (and scammers) is that they promise to hack this rule. They come to you and say: "This rule is for idiots (or the poor). I have figured out the system. There is bread without labor. There is a harvest without sweating.". This promise triggers our "Eden Memory." The most primitive layers of our brain scream, "Yes! I belonged there anyway, I want to return there!". That is exactly why we get scammed. Not because we don't know math. Not because we can't do market analysis. But because deep down, we want to escape that "Cursed Law of Labor.".

Homo Economicus is Dead, Long Live "Bounded Rationality"!

For years in economics books, they told us about a species called "Homo Economicus." Supposedly this species; was a super-intelligent being that always made rational decisions, acted with logic rather than emotions, and calculated profit and loss down to the last penny. Nobel laureate economist Herbert Simon came out in the 1950s and said: "There is no such human. We are creatures equipped with 'Bounded Rationality'.".

Meaning; We cannot process information fully. We are emotional. We are focused on short-term pleasure (apple/money). And most importantly: We prefer the easy over the right.

Didn't the engineer who lost money to Tosuncuk know math? He knew. But at that moment he took off his "Homo Economicus" hat and put on his "Adam Believing in the Alchemist" hat. Because believing was easier than calculating. Believing secreted dopamine; calculating created stress.

Conclusion: Entering the Laboratory

Throughout Chapter 1, we saw this: The problem is not the intelligence of the scammer outside, but the void inside (inside us). We are refugees exiled from Eden, constantly trying to return there (to effortlessness). Alchemists exploit this exact refugee psychology. They sell us fake passports, fake visas, and fake maps of Eden.

Adam ate the apple and was left naked. The investor bought the virtual cow and was left penniless. The fiction is always the same: Wanting a reward without paying the price. Yet the immutable law of life (and economics) is this: Free cheese is only found in a mousetrap.

Now, since we know the Victim (Us), it is time to know the Killer (The Alchemist). We are descending into the dusty shelves and dark laboratories of history. There, by the alembics, among the smells of mercury, we will see the men who prepared the Philosopher's Stone (i.e., the first big lie) for humanity. What was that "Alchemy" that blew even Newton's mind? And how did the alchemists of that day turn into the trading bots of today?

CHAPTER 2
THE GLOW IN THE DARK AND THE FIRST "PUFFERS"

Isaac Newton's Secret Chest and the Bankruptcy of Reason

Year 1727. London.

One of the greatest minds the world has ever seen, Sir Isaac Newton, breathed his last.

The funeral ceremony was held with a splendor fit for kings. He was the symbol of "Reason". He had discovered the law of gravity, unraveled the nature of light, and proven that the universe functioned like a mathematical clock ticking away. For humanity, he marked the end of superstitions and magic, and the beginning of science and enlightenment.

However, after Newton died, when his heirs opened his private chests, they encountered a shocking sight. The thousands of pages of handwritten notes that came out of the chests were not on physics or mathematics. They were full of formulas, Latin ciphers, strange symbols, and recipes on how to obtain the "Philosopher's Stone".

It turns out that rational genius, that cold-blooded scientist, was a passionate alchemist who locked himself in his laboratory at night, inhaling mercury vapors, trying to turn metals into gold. He had inhaled so much mercury that analysis of his hair strands revealed mercury levels 40 times higher than normal.

Now we must ask this question:

How can a man who can calculate the motion of planets believe that he can turn lead into gold? Doesn't intelligence protect one from being deceived?

Answer: No, it doesn't. In fact, because of the condition we call the "Intelligence Paradox", smart people sometimes believe in "big lies" much more easily.

Why Do the Smartest Also Fall For It?

Alchemy is not the trap of fools, but of arrogant minds. Newton believed he could unlock the secret of the universe. He was so confident in himself (his mind) that he thought he could "hack" the laws of nature and find that shortcut hidden by God. This is exactly the profile of modern scam victims.

Those who lose the most money to Ponzi schemes, complex crypto derivatives, or "arbitrage bots" are generally not the illiterate. They are doctors, engineers, bankers, and even finance professors. Because the Alchemist (Scammer) plays to the victim's intelligence, not their ignorance, when approaching them. He presents them with complex charts, technical terms, and opportunities that only smart people can understand.

The victim thinks: "This system is very complex, ordinary people wouldn't understand this, but I do. I am special." This is the trap Newton fell into. The Alchemist empties the victim's wallet by using this intellectual arrogance.

When Newton lost most of his fortune in the stock market (in the South Sea Bubble event), he said that famous quote:

> ***I can calculate the motion of heavenly bodies, but not the madness of people..***

What he actually couldn't calculate was not the madness of people, but the desire for a shortcut within himself.

Entering the Alchemy Laboratory

What was that "Philosopher's Stone" (Lapis Philosophorum) sought by geniuses like Newton?

Was it just a stone that turned metal into gold?

No.

That stone was also the ultimate power that granted immortality (Elixir of Life) and bestowed Divine Knowledge upon its owner. It was the laboratory equivalent of the apple Adam bit.

However, while "true seekers" like Newton worked in the laboratory, a completely different group had sprung up outside. History's first professional scammers. The public called them "Puffers". Why? Because the bellows they used to stoke the coal in the furnace constantly made a "Puff, puff" sound. But what they were actually puffing were lies.

These men went to the palaces of kings, wore fancy robes, and claimed to have a secret powder in their hands. They said, "Give me some gold, and I will multiply it with this powder." And kings, just like today's CEOs, wanted to believe this lie. Because the Alchemist's promise is the same in every age: *Effortless gain, effortless power.*

Now, we will leave Newton's dark laboratory and take a closer look at the methods of these "Puffers". Because the sleight-of-hand techniques they used are the ancestors of the techniques used today on Wall Street or Instagram.

Welcome. This is where reason ends and desire begins.

The Alchemist's Trick Box: Virus Updated

If you were a "Puffer" (Fake Alchemist) living in the 17th century and wanted to convince the king that you could "turn lead into gold", you didn't need to know chemistry. You just needed a bit of "sleight of hand" and a good theatrical talent.

Historical records show how creative the "viruses" (tricks) these men used were. The most famous trick was the "Hollow Stirring Rod". The alchemist appears before the king. He throws the worthless lead into the cauldron. Then he takes a wooden stirring rod in his hand and starts stirring the mixture. The king watches carefully. But what the king doesn't know is this: The rod is hollow inside, and it has been pre-filled with real gold dust. The tip of the rod is sealed with wax that melts with heat.

As the alchemist stirs the mixture in the hot cauldron, the wax melts, and the gold dust inside the rod pours into the cauldron. The alchemist says "Hocus Pocus!", empties the cauldron, and voila! There is gleaming gold at the bottom. The king is in shock. He has seen it with his own eyes. There can be no trick (!). And he immediately opens his treasury to the alchemist: "Sell me this formula!" At that moment, the king actually bought the sleight of hand, not the gold.

Modern Times: The "F12" Key Replaced the Wand

Now let's teleport to the present, to the digital world of the 2020s. Human hardware (operating system) is still the same: Believing one's eyes. Our brain operates with the bias "What I see is real!".

The Postmodern Alchemist (Crypto Influencer or Forex Guru) no longer uses a hollow rod. His new wand is the "Inspect Element" key in the internet browser.

A scammer who actually has 100 TL in his bank account can right-click on the browser and play with the codes to show that figure as 1,000,000 TL on the screen. Then he takes a screenshot of this, posts it on Instagram, and writes underneath: "Profit from today's trade. Are you still going to continue to suffer in your salaried job?"

Whatever the king in 1600 felt looking at the gold at the bottom of that cauldron; the youth in 2025 feels the same when looking at that screenshot: Proof.

"The guy is making money, bro, I saw the receipt!"

No, you didn't. You only saw the illusion he wanted to show you.

- The old alchemist would hide gold dust under his fingernail.
- The new alchemist trades on a Demo Account (virtual money) and shows it as a "Real Account" (real mon-

ey). The methods (viruses) have been updated, but the system's vulnerability is always the same: Visual Evidence Fallacy.

The Second Rule of the Alchemist: The Illusion of Complexity

So why doesn't the king or the modern investor say, "Can I check the rod?" or "Let's connect live to your account and see"? Because the Alchemist surrounds his victim with a "Wall of Incomprehensibility".

Look at the notes of the old alchemists: Dragon's blood, Phoenix feather, Latin prayers, astrological charts... They would create such a complex ritual that the victim would be embarrassed to ask, "Is he tricking me?". Because if he asked, he would look ignorant.

Today, technical analysis charlatans build the same wall. Fibonacci sequences, Elliott waves, Bollinger bands, RSI indicators... There are so many lines, so many terms on the screen!

The victim thinks to himself: "These complex charts can't be a lie. This guy is a genius." However, most of those charts are nothing more than the show in the alchemist's smoky laboratory.

Real wealthy people like Warren Buffett make their investments with a logic simple enough for a 10-year-old child to understand. The Alchemist, on the other hand, deliberately complicates the simple so that "his secret cannot be reached". Because complexity is the best mask for incompetence.

Gravity Is Unforgiving: The Bankruptcy of a Genius and the Gallows

In movies, the villains, scammers, or thieves usually escape to a tropical island with the money they stole and enjoy life sipping their cocktails. This is a lie sold to us by Hollywood.

The script of real life is much more ruthless and fair. Throughout history, the fate of those who pursued the "Philosopher's Stone", that is, effortless wealth (both the scammers and the greedy victims), has almost never changed: *Either prison, misery, or the gallows.*

Because the universe has a law of justice as certain as the laws of thermodynamics: Everything whose balance is disturbed settles back into place harshly.

Newton's "Apocalypse" in the Stock Market

Let's go back to Isaac Newton. He couldn't turn lead into gold in the alchemy laboratory, but in 1720, he thought he could turn paper into gold in the London Stock Exchange.

At that time, there was a company called the *"South Sea Company"*. Just like some tech stocks or cryptocurrencies today, this company promised infinite profit. Everyone was buying these stocks.

Newton, as a rational genius, initially acted cautiously. He bought the shares, made a nice profit, and sold them. He put millions of dollars in today's money into his pocket. "Okay," he said, "I'm smart, I won and got out."

But then what happened?

FOMO (Fear of Missing Out), the greatest weapon of the alchemists, kicked in. After selling, Newton saw that the shares went up even further. He watched his friends, whom he found much "stupider" than himself, earn more than him.

His arrogance defeated his mind.

Saying, "I am Newton, I can calculate where the market will turn," he reinvested his entire fortune, even borrowing more, at the very peak of the shares.

And the inevitable end: The bubble burst.

The law of gravity applied in the stock market too. Everything that goes up must come down. Newton lost approximately 4-5 million dollars in today's money. He was left penniless. The smartest man in the world had lost his health (with mercury) trying to be an alchemist in the laboratory, and his fortune trying to be an alchemist in the stock market.

Divine justice taught him this: Intelligence, if it doesn't overcome greed, drags its owner to disaster.

The End of Charlatans: Gold-Plated Gallows

And what about those "Puffers?", the fake alchemists who deceived kings?

They didn't win either.

History books write that in Middle Age and Renaissance Europe, special gallows were set up for charlatans who defrauded palaces by claiming "I make gold". These gallows, ironically, were painted with gold gilding.

Justice was telling them: *"You loved gold very much, you poisoned people with your lie. Now you will die on a rope painted in the color of that gold you love so much."*

This rule has not changed today either:

- **Charles Ponzi:** He scammed millions of dollars, but died in a charity hospital ward in Rio de Janeiro, penniless and blind. Even his funeral was paid for by the state.
- **Bernie Madoff:** The biggest stock market fraudster in history. He lived in luxury, but spent the last years of his life in a prison cell, his son having committed suicide, his family torn apart, and having lost all his reputation.
- **Tosuncuks and Crypto Kings:** Look at the headlines today. Most of those posing in luxury cars are now either living a life on the run (which is a prison) or behind iron bars.

Conclusion: You Reap What You Sow

As we close Chapter 2, we must note this truth:

"Alchemy is a rebellion against nature. It is an attempt to get results without putting in effort. And nature (or Divine Justice) never leaves rebellions against itself unpunished."

In the short term, it may look like "The Alchemist is winning". They may look happy on Instagram, on luxury yachts, in plazas. But the end of the movie never changes. As Newton said: "Every action has an equal and opposite reaction."

If you send lies and greed (action) to the universe, the universe returns it to you as destruction and bankruptcy (reaction). This is the common law of physics, economics, and theology.

CHAPTER 3
FLOWERS, CHAINS, AND THE GREATER FOOL THEORY

History's Most Expensive Bulb and Waiting for the Greater Fool

Year 1637. Amsterdam.

The heart of global trade, the capital of wealth.

There are scents of spices in the ports, and a heavy scent of "opportunity" on the streets. The Dutch were known as the most rational, mercantile, and calculating nation of the world at that time.

However, this rational nation was caught in a strange spell in those days. The alchemists were in gardens this time, not laboratories. They hadn't turned lead into gold, but they had managed to make a plant pulled from the earth more valuable than gold.

Our topic: The Tulip.

Today, it may look like an ordinary flower bought on Valentine's Day. But in the world of that day, the Tulip, especially the "Semper Augustus" variety with red-and-white flame patterns on its petals, was not just a flower.

It was a ticket dropped from heaven.

It was status.

And most importantly, it was the first "Crypto Asset" history had ever seen.

The Million-Dollar Breakfast

To understand the magnitude of this craze (Tulip Mania), let's look at a tragicomic story recorded in Charles Mackay's notes.

A wealthy Dutch merchant offers a herring to a sailor who arrived at the port for a business meeting, as a snack while waiting. On the merchant's table, resting on a velvet cloth, is something that looks like an onion. The sailor thinks this is a dry onion that will go well with the fish. He takes it, peels it, and eats it with pleasure. The merchant suffers a heart attack upon seeing the scene when he returns to the room. The sailor, thinking it was an onion, had just eaten a Semper Augustus tulip bulb, the value of which was equal to the most luxurious canal house in Amsterdam (millions of dollars in today's money).

For the sailor, the value of that thing was simply to satisfy his stomach (Use Value). For the merchant, however, that thing was a fortune (Exchange Value).

This is exactly where Alchemy comes into play: When the connection between the true value (an onion) of an object (Tulip, Bitcoin, NFT, Land) and the imaginary value ascribed to it (a fortune) breaks, "Magic" emerges.

Did the Dutch pay this money because they loved tulips so much?

No.

Nobody was buying that tulip to plant it in their garden and say, "How nice it smells".

The Greater Fool Theory

People paid the price of a house for a bulb because they trusted the most ruthless and valid theory in financial history: *The Greater Fool Theory.*

This theory allows us to read the mind of an alchemist (speculator). It says:

"I am aware that I paid an illogical price (100 units) for this bulb. This is a foolish move. But I know that a 'Greater Fool' who comes after me will pay 200 units for this. That's why I am making a profit."

This is the market version of the feeling Adam felt when reaching for the apple. Adam wanted the apple not to eat (use) it, but to "transform" (level up in status). The Dutch also bought the tulip not to smell it, but to transform it into wealth. Everyone was trying not to be that "Greatest Fool" at the end of the chain. Everyone was planning to pass the hot potato (the tulip bulb) in their hands to someone else, take their profit, and run.

The Alchemist's New Laboratory: The Stock Market

Alchemists used to work in dark basements. In the Netherlands, they moved to stock markets called Collegium, set up in the back rooms of taverns. Here, not even the tulip itself changed hands anymore.

The tulip itself was underground. People were buying and selling papers written on tulips that would bloom in the future (Futures Contracts). This was "Selling Thin Air". And air is lighter than gold, but it rises faster than gold.

Those days in Amsterdam taverns, legends circulated that a shoeshine boy was richer than a nobleman. "Did you hear? Hans the tailor sold his entire shop, bought a Viceroy bulb, and is now having a chateau built!" These gossips (The Whisper Network) canceled the society's rational mind (Frontal Cortex). Herd psychology kicked in. Nobody was saying "This is an onion!" anymore. Everyone was saying "This is an opportunity!". Just like a digital token (Memecoin) with no function reaching a billion-dollar volume today.

People haven't changed. Only "Coin" took the place of the tulip, and "Telegram Groups" took the place of the tavern, and everyone continued to dance, hoping they were not the "Greatest Fool" in that room. Until the music stopped...

When the Music Stops: Nigredo and the Sound of Silence

February 3, 1637. The city of Haarlem. This was the heart of the Tulip Exchange. Every day, millions of guilders (Dutch currency) worth of transactions were made, and fortunes changed hands.

That morning, a routine auction began. The auctioneer shouted the starting price for a rare bulb in his hand (perhaps a *Viceroy* or *Admiral Van der Eijck*). Under normal circumstances, this price should have doubled or tripled in seconds, with merchants crushing each other to increase the bid.

But that morning, something strange happened.

Silence...

Nobody raised their hand. The auctioneer was surprised. He lowered the price a bit. Silence again... He lowered it a bit more. That heavy, suffocating silence in the hall continued. At that moment, the same terrible pain pierced the stomachs of everyone in the hall at the same time. That silence was the end of an era. At that moment, everyone realized the same truth: The "Greater Fool" had not arrived. The last link of the chain had broken. And those papers in their hands were no longer a fortune, but merely pieces of paper.

Panic: If Everyone Tries to Exit the Door at the Same Time

In the alchemists' laboratory, the "Golden Phase" (Rubedo) had ended, and the "Black Phase" (Nigredo) had begun.

Nigredo is decay, dissolution, and chaos. For the alchemist, this is a spiritual confrontation, but for the investor, this is a financial death.

That silence spread like a virus from Haarlem to Amsterdam, and from there to Rotterdam. The whisper network this time carried disaster, not wealth:

"No buyers! Nobody is buying!"

"Loss Aversion", the most primitive fear of human psychology, kicked in. Noblemen who said "I will never sell, I will buy a chateau with this bulb" just a day ago, started running in the streets a day later begging, "Whatever you give, just take this from me". But the market is ruthless. If there is no buyer, the price is "zero".

Million-worth bills turned into toilet paper.

Hans the tailor, who woke up rich yesterday, was today a bankrupt who lost not only his shop, but also his house, his reputation, and his future.

Alchemy Backfires: Turning from Gold to Lead

Remember that metaphor we mentioned at the beginning of the chapter: "Here lead turns into gold". During the week the Tulip Mania burst, this process worked in reverse. People looked at that magical asset in their hands and saw only a wrinkled, odorless, muddy onion. The spell was broken. The princess had turned back into a frog.

This awakening was so harsh that the Dutch canals that winter did not just freeze from the cold; they were filled with the corpses of merchants who committed suicide. The rich became poor, the poor were condemned to starvation. The society's sense of trust (Social Trust) was shattered. Nobody trusted anyone else's deed or word anymore. Because the "Effortless Wealth" promised by the Alchemists had rotted the moral fabric of society.

In a society where everyone is a gambler, nobody wants to be a baker and bake bread. And when the bubble bursts, neither bread nor money is left in hand.

Lesson: Being Able to Say "The Emperor Has No Clothes"

It is easy to look back from today and laugh at the Dutch. We say, "Would anyone pay that much money for an onion?". But in 2021, when "Dogecoin", produced merely as an internet joke and having no project or function, surpassed the century-old automotive giant Honda in market value... Did we do anything different?

No.

We were also in that auction hall in Haarlem. We also thought the Greater Fool would be there forever.

The Tulip Mania teaches us this:

If the price of an asset is based solely on the belief of how much others will pay for it, it is not an investment, it is a gamble.

And in gambling, the house (i.e., the laws of nature) always wins. When the music stops, the one left standing, unable to find a chair (true value) in their hands, is us.

Now, let's step out from among these ruins, these rotten onions, and bankrupt lives. History awaits that "Evil Genius" who will take this scattered amateur fraud and pour it into an elegant system, a mathematical formula.

Next up is the greatest illusionist of modern times: *Charles Ponzi.*

Mr. Alchemist Takes the Stage: Charles Ponzi

Let's go about 300 years after the tulip crisis in the Netherlands, to the America of the 1920s. The Jazz Age, the madness before the Great Depression, and those "American Dream" years where everyone dreamed of getting rich.

In the streets of Boston, wandering with only a few dollars in his pocket, was a short man of Italian descent: Charles Ponzi. Ponzi claimed he had found the formula the alchemists had sought for centuries (turning lead into gold) not with chemistry, but with "Arbitrage".

How the "System" Worked? (Or Didn't Work)

What Ponzi discovered was the price difference between International Reply Coupons (IRC). Theoretically, the system was this:

- The currency of post-war countries in Europe was worthless. There, a reply coupon could be bought for 1 cent.
- When this coupon was cashed in America, it was worth 6 cents.
- Ponzi told people: *"Give me your money, I will buy cheap coupons from Europe on your behalf, and sell them expensive here. Let me give you 50% profit in 45 days, 100% profit in 90 days."*

In a world where banks gave 5% interest a year, the promise of 100% profit in 90 days was as mesmerizing as the "Eternity promised to Adam".

Mathematically, this transaction (Arbitrage) seemed possible. But in practice, it was impossible. Because the amount of coupons needed to distribute that much profit was even more than the total number of coupons in the world! It would require Titanic-loads of coupons to be transported.

But nobody asked, "How will the logistics work?".

Because Ponzi was the best "Confidence Merchant" history had ever seen.

Paying the Old Investor with the New

Ponzi actually never traded any coupons. What he did was set up that famous Ponzi Scheme (Pyramid Scheme) known by his name today:

He was giving the money he took from Ahmet to Mehmet as a profit share. This is the peak of financial alchemy. There is no production (no lead), no trade (no labor), only money circulation. But as people got their money back (or thought they did), the legend grew.

Ponzi became so popular that the police had to manage the queue in front of his office. People were crushing each other to give their accumulated life savings (baby formula money, retirement bonuses) to this magician.

Ponzi was collecting 1 million dollars a day (a massive fortune in today's money). He was seen as a modern Robin Hood. Banks (the old order) were exploiting the public, while Ponzi (the new order/alchemist) was making the public rich.

Just like crypto scammers today badmouthing banks by saying Decentralized Finance and selling their own tokens. The rhetoric is always the same: "We are against the system, we are on the side of the people."

The Collapse and Modern Heirs

However, as in every alchemy experiment, Nigredo (Collapse) was inevitable here too. A journalist (Boston Post) made a simple calculation: "There aren't this many coupons in the world. Where does this man find the money?". The moment the question was asked, the spell was broken.

Investors came asking for their money. Ponzi paid the first ones who came (to refresh trust). But the crowd grew. No money was left in the vault. And Charles Ponzi tumbled from a multi-million dollar fortune into a prison cell, and finally to a penniless death in a charity ward in Brazil.

Today's Ponzis: The Name Changed, The Logic is the Same

Charles Ponzi died, but his spirit permeated every corner of the modern economy. Today, systems under the name of Network Marketing saying "Bring a member and win"; Crypto sites saying we are doing "Cloud Mining"; all are Ponzi's grandchildren. The product (detergent, holiday package, digital coin) is merely a decor. The real product is the new sucker who enters the system.

In the alchemist's laboratory, the rule is this: The last one in turns off the light and pays the bill.

Conclusion: The Mathematics of Greed

In this chapter stretching from tulip bulbs to Charles Ponzi, we saw this:

People get into things they know (or feel) are illogical just because others are winning. Separating from the herd is scarier than losing. Alchemists combine our fear of being alone (FOMO) and our desire for a shortcut (Greed), and sell us a dream with our own money. And we are always ready to buy that dream.

CHAPTER 4
THE ALCHEMIST'S MIRROR AND THE ART OF PRETENDING

New York's Fake Princess: Anna Delvey's Magic Mirror

Alchemists of old times would lock themselves in their laboratories, their hands covered in coal soot, inhaling mercury to search for the Philosopher's Stone. Their business was with matter.

Postmodern Alchemists, on the other hand, do not get their hands dirty. Their laboratory is the 6-inch shiny phone screens. What they are looking for is not gold; it is likes, followers, and reputation. Because in the 21st century, these three can be cashed out faster than gold.

In the past, there was the motto "Either appear as you are, or be as you appear" (Rumi).

Today, there is only one rule: "Fake It Till You Make It". The brightest and most audacious example of this new type of alchemy was the daughter of a Russian truck driver in her 20s, who played the New York high society like a fiddle at the end of the 2010s: Anna Sorokin. Or by the name everyone knows her: Anna Delvey.

The Power of Non-Existent Money

Anna Delvey's story starts like a modern fairy tale but ends like a horror movie.

She didn't have a dime in her pocket. Her father wasn't a wealthy German businessman. She didn't have a 60 million dollar trust fund. But Anna had discovered the modern world's biggest vulnerability:

People were so ready to believe what they saw that nobody questioned the reality (the bank account).

Anna's alchemy was this: She stayed in luxury hotels, ate at the most expensive restaurants, and distributed 100-dollar tips to waiters (with money not in her bank account).

The clothes she wore, her posture, that arrogant and nonchalant attitude... Everything about her screamed "I am rich and I am above these rules". And an incredible thing happened: The system believed her.

Because they believed her, luxury hotels were embarrassed to say "Your credit card isn't working". They said, "Such a rich woman will surely pay, there must be a mistake". Bankers tried to give her multi-million dollar loans.

Social Arbitrage: Turning Nothingness into Status

Charles Ponzi claimed to take advantage of the price difference (arbitrage) between reply coupons. Anna Delvey, however, did "Social Arbitrage". The mechanism she used was a mirror. She would look at the people across from her (bankers, hotels, socialites) and reflect back to them what they wanted to see, namely wealth, youth, and audacity.

Anna was the physical embodiment of the first lie the Devil whispered to Adam, the promise of "Eat the forbidden fruit, be like God". She gave the people around her this message simply by her presence: "If you stand next to me, you too will get a share of this glimmer". The smartest, shrewdest bankers in New York fell for this simple illusion, just like Newton did. Because Anna was not selling them a business plan, she was selling a "Lifestyle" and the rule in this postmodern alchemy is this: If enough people believe you are rich, you really start to get rich. (Until the bills cannot be paid and the bubble bursts).

Anna eventually got caught and went to prison. But today she is out of prison, still living in luxury, giving interviews, and even participating in a dance competition. Why? Because thanks to the alchemy she achieved, she is no longer just a scammer; she is a brand.

Anna Delvey taught us this: If you hold the mirror at the right angle, you can make the emptiness behind you (poverty) look like a giant palace (wealth).

Now we will take this mirror from Anna and turn it to the phone screens we never drop from our hands all day. Next up are those who are each a little Anna Delvey in their own right.

Rented Ferraris and Digital Narcotics

Anna Delvey had to be physically there, wear those clothes, and stay in those hotels to deceive people. This was an exhausting and expensive job. The new version of Postmodern Alchemy is much more efficient (scalable). There is no longer a need for physical presence. There are only pixels.

Most of the success stories (Success Porn) we see on social media today are a production set that would make Hollywood studios jealous.

Private Jet Studios and Hourly Wealth

Did you know that there are photo studios designed like the inside of a private jet in Los Angeles and Moscow? These studios do not fly. It is just a decor sitting on the ground. But they can be rented for $50 an hour. When you see that young entrepreneur (Alchemist) on Instagram saying *"Are you still working 9 to 5? I set up this system and now I'm above the clouds"*, he is actually sitting on a plastic chair in a windowless room in the backstreets of Los Angeles at that moment. But your brain cannot distinguish this. Your brain (that Dutch brain that paid a fortune for a tulip bulb) believes in that leather seat, that champagne glass, and those clouds it sees. This is the "Rented Status" industry.

Luxury cars in Dubai are not just rented to be driven. Most of the time, they are rented just to stand next to and take photos. That car is not a means of transportation, it is bait. The photo taken in front of that car is the packaging of the training set or investment advice the alchemist will sell.

The Alchemist tells you: "If you want to ride in this car, you must buy the secret I am selling." Whereas the truth is this: He desperately needs you to buy that training in order to pay the installment on that car. This is a digital Ponzi cycle.

The Alchemy of Filters: Lead Faces, Golden Visages

Not just money, but beauty is also a subject of alchemy now. Medieval alchemists were looking for the perfect metal (gold). Today's human, on the other hand, is looking for the perfect self. Filters are the Philosopher's Stone of the modern era. You press a button; fatigue disappears, the skin shines, the nose shrinks, the lips become fuller. That flawed/mortal human in the mirror (Lead) turns into a flawless/eternal deity on the screen (Gold). This might look like an innocent game. But its psychological cost is very heavy.

People get so used to their filtered states that they start to hate their real faces in the mirror. The doors of plastic surgeons are full of patients holding their own filtered photos and saying “Make me look like this”. This condition is called “Snapchat Dysmorphia” in psychology.

The Alchemist (Technology) promised us “A better you”, but actually created “A you who hates themselves”..

Digital Narcotics: The Dopamine Cycle

So, why are we so addicted to these lies? Why do we continue to watch even though we know that Influencer is not really that happy, and that product doesn’t really work that well? Because Alchemists figured out our brain’s weakness very well: Dopamine.

Every “Like” sparks a small reward signal in the brain. Every “Scroll” is like pulling the lever of a slot machine: “I wonder what’s next? Something beautiful? Something funny?”

Social media companies hired the best behavioral scientists to design these platforms like casinos. Their goal is not to inform us; it is to keep us in front of that screen (in the laboratory). Because in their alchemy, the raw material is us. Our attention, our time, and our envy are the lead they turn into gold.

Alchemy in the Ballot Box: Post-Truth and the Allure of the Lie

Anna Delvey deceived New York hotels. Tosuncuk deceived 80 thousand people. Charles Ponzi deceived all of Boston. But Political Alchemists (Populist Leaders) can hypnotize millions, even entire nations, with a single "Story". What politicians are looking for in the laboratory is not to turn lead into gold. Their goal is to turn the fears and longings of the society into votes.And in the 21st century, they don't need the truth to do this job.

Welcome to the "Post-Truth" era.

"Truth" is Now a Boring Detail!

In 2016, the Oxford Dictionary selected *Post-Truth* as the word of the year. Its definition was this: "Relating to or denoting circumstances in which objective facts are less influential in shaping public opinion than appeals to emotion and personal belief." In other words, it says: Whether something is true or not doesn't matter anymore. What matters is how that lie makes you feel.

The Alchemist takes the podium and says: "The economy is flying! We are making the world jealous!" A rational citizen (Homo Economicus) looks at the money in pocket, looks at the price tag in the market, and says "This is a lie".

But the "Post-Truth Citizen" (Emotional Human) chooses to believe this lie. Because believing is more comfortable than facing the bitter truth.

When the Alchemist tells them, *"You are not poor, you are a long-suffering soldier of a great cause"*; this lie strokes the citizen's ego. It transforms their poverty (Lead) into a sacred sacrifice (Gold). This is the greatest alchemy trick in history: *Turning pain into pride.*

The Alchemy of Nostalgia: The Lie of the "Good Old Days"

The favorite product of political alchemists is "Nostalgia". Wherever you go in the world, the slogans of populist leaders are always the same:

"Make America Great Again!"

"Great France!"

"The Ottoman Spirit"

"The Return of the Roman Empire"

They all promise a return to a "Golden Age" that allegedly existed in the past (but actually never existed).

Why?

Because the future is uncertain and scary. The past is safe.

Instead of solving today's problems (inflation, immigration, unemployment), the Alchemist sells the masses the dream of the past.

There is no difference in terms of method between the Devil telling Adam *"You will return to Eden"* and the politician telling the voter *"We will return to those glorious old days".* Both are selling back the Lost Paradise.

Why Do Lies Spread at the Speed of Light?

Let's remember Mark Twain's magnificent quote: "A lie can travel halfway around the world while the truth is putting on its shoes."

In the age of social media, this quote has turned into a scientific law. According to a study conducted by MIT (Massachusetts Institute of Technology), fake news spreads 6 times faster than true news on Twitter (X).

Why?

Because the truth is boring. The truth is complex. The truth is gray. Lies, on the other hand, are exciting, clear, black and white.

If you say "The cause of the economic crisis is the interest-inflation imbalance", nobody retweets it. If you say "The cause of the economic crisis is the secret game of foreign powers", you get thousands of likes. The Alchemist knows this algorithm. That's why they never talk about data. They always talk about enemies, conspiracies, and grand schemes. Because they know that the masses don't want an explanation; the masses want a witch to blame and a hero to worship.

Conclusion: The Face in the Mirror

There is only one truth we see in this chapter stretching from Anna Delvey to Instagram filters, and from there to the political squares:

We are not being deceived.

We are becoming accomplices to those fancy lies...

The people around Anna Delvey knew deep down that she wasn't rich, but they didn't want the party to end. The follower on Instagram knows that the influencer is not really that happy, but they like looking at that dream. The voter knows those promises won't be kept, but listening to that "Great Powerful Country" fairy tale gives them peace.

The Alchemist's Mirror doesn't actually show us the lie. The Alchemist's Mirror shows us our own weaknesses. And as long as we look into that mirror and say "How beautiful I am", alchemists will continue to win.

CHAPTER 5
THE BAZAAR OF THE SOUL AND MODERN SHAMANS

Marrying Quantum and Spiritual Materialism

Modern humans working in plazas, earning good money, driving a nice car, and holding the latest model phone... From the outside, they look successful. They have reached that status promised by the Alchemists (the Anna Delveys). But when they lay their head on the pillow at night, they feel a huge, dark hole in the middle of their chest. They have earned money but haven't found peace. They have followers but no friends. They have everything but they have nothing.

This emptiness is the new mine for the Alchemists. It is the oldest rule in history: Where there is demand, supply will follow. Modern humans are starving for "meaning," and to feed this hunger, Alchemists have developed a new formula in their laboratories: "Fast Enlightenment."

"I Am Enlightened, It's Your Turn (VAT Included)"

In the past, attaining enlightenment or finding peace required years of suffering, seclusion, patience, and taming the ego. The journey of a dervish, a monk, or a philosopher would take a lifetime. But modern humans don't have the time to wait a lifetime. They want everything "right here, right now."

- They want their hamburger fast (Fast Food).
- They want their fashion fast (Fast Fashion).
- Therefore, they also want their peace fast (Fast Spirit).

İşte bu yüzden sahneye "Modern Şamanlar", "Yaşam Koçları" ve "Kuantum Terapistleri" çıkar.

That is why "Modern Shamans," "Life Coaches," and "Quantum Therapists" appear on the stage. They tell you: "You don't need to suffer for 40 years. Come to our Inner Awakening Camp this weekend (price is $5,000), and let us upload the secret of the universe to you. Return to work on Monday having reached Nirvana." This promise is no different from Charles Ponzi's 100% profit promise. Both play on the desire to "get results without paying the price" (effortless gain)

Tibetan meditation master Chögyam Trungpa gave a wonderful name to this situation: "Spiritual Materialism." That is; using spirituality not to destroy the ego, but to inflate the ego even further.

- "I am more aware than you."
- "My chakras are more open than yours."
- "You are still in the 3rd dimension, I have moved to the 5th dimension."

These sentences stem from the same root of arrogance as the sentence "My car is more expensive than yours." Only the decor has changed; "aura" has replaced money.

Word Games: The Quantum Refuge

The biggest trick of this bazaar is to use the most complex and incomprehensible field of science, namely Quantum Physics, as a marketing mask. Quantum physics studies the uncertain behavior of subatomic particles. And yes, weird things happen there. But Alchemists (Charlatans) take this weirdness and use it as a cover for the absurdities of daily life.

- Did your lover leave you? *"Your quantum entanglement broke."*
- Do you need money? *"You didn't send the right frequency to the universe."*
- Are things going badly? *"You have an energy blockage; come and let's solve it for 500 TL."*

If Heisenberg or Schrödinger were to rise from their graves and see these quantum life coaches, they would probably die again of grief. Because the Alchemist is selling a word they don't understand (quantum) to a desperate person as if it were a scientific miracle. The logic here is this: "This is so scientific that you wouldn't understand it, but if you pay the money, it works." Remember? This is the exact same tactic as the Latin formulas used by the puffers of Newton's era in Chapter 2. Yesterday it was Latin, today it is Quantum.

Santiago's Treasure and the Wrong Map

One cannot talk about alchemy without mentioning Paulo Coelho's cult novel, *The Alchemist.* In that book, the Andalusian shepherd Santiago hits the road to search for his personal legend (life purpose). Coelho's famous sentence is engraved in the hearts of millions: "When you want something, all the universe conspires in helping you to achieve it." This is a tremendous motivation for a fairy-tale hero. However, in the real world, this sentence has turned into a dangerous weapon in the hands of Postmodern Alchemists.

The Alchemist in Coelho's book does not give Santiago fish, nor does he teach him how to fish; he merely advises him to look inside himself. The treasure is the long and difficult journey itself that Santiago embarks on. Today's Instagram Alchemists, on the other hand, distort this philosophy. They tell you; "You don't need to go on a journey, you don't need to suffer, you don't need to go to the Pyramids of Egypt." "You just ask (and pay the fee), and I will bring the universe's cooperation to your feet."

Coelho's hero Santiago worked for years, was robbed, beaten, and matured to reach the treasure. Modern victims, however, want to reach Santiago's finale by sitting where they are and sending messages to the universe. The difference is this:

- Coelho's Alchemy is a journey of inner transformation.
- Modern Alchemy is an external transfer (money transfer) trap.

If someone promises you Santiago's ending without suffering Santiago's ordeal; know that they are not a sage, but a merchant.

The Universe Is Not an Order Hotline!

At the foundation of these teachings (New Age movements) lies a dangerous narcissism: The Law of Attraction (The Secret). They tell us: *"The universe is like a waiter waiting to fulfill your wishes. You just ask, imagine, and the universe will give it to you."* This is the pinnacle of human arrogance. It is reducing the entire cosmos, billions of galaxies, to the order hotline of our own little ego.

According to this thought;

- If you are rich, it's because you radiate good energy. (Good for you).
- If you are poor, sick, or a child born in the middle of a war; it's because you radiate bad energy (or you attracted it to yourself).

This perspective is not only foolish, but it is also ruthless. Because it blames the victim. It says, "You asked for it, you attracted it." True spirituality (religious or philosophical) begins with humans accepting their "smallness" (helplessness) in the face of the universe. The spirituality of Alchemists, on the other hand, begins with the claim that humans are the "Masters of the Universe." And this is the very same first lie whispered to Adam: "*You will be like God.*"

The Title Deed to Heaven and the "Fireproof Shroud" Market

History books tell us that in Medieval Europe, the Catholic Church sold Indulgences (Land in Heaven/Certificate of Forgiveness). The system is simple: Did you commit a sin? Are you afraid of Hell? Make a donation to the church, let the Pope speak to God on your behalf, and shorten your time in purgatory.

It sounds so absurd to us today, doesn't it? But in the Turkey of the 2020s (or other parts of the world), we saw fireproof shrouds being sold on television screens. "Whoever wears this shroud will not suffer the torment of the grave; the fire of hell will not burn them." The name of the product has changed (fabric instead of paper), but the mechanism has remained exactly the same: The Trade of Fear.

The Alchemist's Greatest Trump Card: Guaranteed Salvation

The Alchemist, who is a merchant of religion, knows their customer's greatest fear (death and the afterlife). And they sell them a policy that no insurance company in the world could provide: A Guarantee of Eternal Salvation.

Normally, for a religious person, salvation is between hope and fear (khawf and raja). There is no guarantee, there is effort, there is prayer. This uncertainty is hard for the human ego. Humans want "certainty."

This is where the Alchemist steps in: "Follow me, join my cult, wear the ring I sell, or read the book I wrote... I am your guarantor. I will hold your hand on the Sirat bridge."

This promise is much bigger than Charles Ponzi's "100% profit" promise. Because Ponzi only promises to save your money, this Alchemist promises to save your soul. What they ask in return (money, obedience, votes) even seems cheap to the customer. Think about it, if the price of escaping eternal hell is just the cost of a shroud or unconditional obedience to a sheikh, this is a "rational" exchange! The Alchemist uses that immense arbitrage (value difference) once again.

Transfer of Will: "Escape from Freedom"

So, why do educated, sane people enter these structures? Why do they kneel before a person and surrender their minds to them? Erich Fromm calls this "Escape from Freedom."

Making decisions is exhausting. Taking responsibility for one's life, thinking "What did I do right, what did I do wrong?" is a heavy burden. The Alchemist (Sheikh/Guru/Leader) offers their disciple a comfortable proposition: "Don't think. Thinking is hard for you. Give your will to me. I will think for you, I will decide for you. You just obey and find peace."

This is a mental narcotic. The person who invested in Çiftlik Bank wanted to get rid of the burden of working. The person who gives their mind to the cult alchemist wants to get rid of the burden of responsibility. Both are shortcuts. One is an economic shortcut, the other is a theological shortcut. And at the end of both lies frustration. Because you cannot go to heaven with someone else's mind, and you cannot get rich with someone else's money.

"The Chosen One" Marketing

At the center of these structures (whether a New Age cult or a religious community), there is always a chosen leader. That leader is the "Mahdi," the "Imam of the Universe," the "Universal Energy Channel." They are not an ordinary human. They are the sole authorized dealer between God (or the Universe) and the servant.

In the technology world, this is called "Vendor Lock-in" (Dependence on the Seller). If you enter the Apple ecosystem, it becomes difficult to use Samsung. The Alchemist also builds their own ecosystem: "The truth is only with us. Outsiders (other communities, other people) are heretics. If you leave us, you will perish."

This wall of fear keeps the customer (disciple) inside. Questioning is forbidden. Because questioning voids the "guarantee."

Conclusion: Alchemy Backfires

Closing Chapter 5, we see that; what is sold in the Bazaar of the Soul is not spirituality, but "Spiritual Narcotics." True faith liberates humans, while the faith of Alchemists enslaves them. True faith asks "Do you not use your intellect?"; Alchemists say "Do not question, obey!"

We started with the story of Adam, and we have come to this point. What did the Devil say to Adam? "You will become an angel." What does the merchant of religion say? "If you are with me, you will be the chosen one." The lie never changed. It only changed costumes. Sometimes it wore a suit (Banker), sometimes it wore a robe (Sheikh), sometimes it wore yoga pants (Guru). But all of them held the same poisonous apple: "Heaven attained without paying the price."

The Lonely Hearts Club and Placebo Priests

When sociologists define the modern era, they give a terrifying statistic: We are living in the most connected (thanks to the internet) but the loneliest period in human history. In plazas, in metropolises, among millions of people, we are all alone. When we return home in the evening, there is no tribe waiting for us. There is only Netflix and a dull screen light.

This is where the Alchemist (Cult Leader, Guru, or Coach) builds their laboratory, right on top of this loneliness crisis. Their actual product is not spirituality. What they sell is the feeling of belonging.

Love Bombing

Imagine someone newly entering a cult or a spiritual group. The moment they walk through the door, they are met with an attention they have never seen before. Everyone smiles at them, hugs them, and says, "Welcome, we were waiting for you, you are very special." In psychology, this is called "Love Bombing."

For the modern human shivering from loneliness, this warmth acts like a drug. Their brain secretes oxytocin (attachment hormone) and dopamine. The person thinks: "This must be heaven. Because the outside world is very cold, but here it is so warm."

After creating this addiction, the Alchemist slowly begins to issue the invoice. First, they want your money, then your time, and finally your will. To not lose that warmth, you give everything, even if you know it's illogical. Because returning to the loneliness outside is scarier than enduring the exploitation inside.

Placebo Priests: Dumbo's Feather

But what about those who say "It works!"? Those sincere people who say, "Master, I wore that stone and my headache went away" or "That sheikh touched me and my depression ended"? Are they lying? No, they are not lying. They are healing. But what heals them is not the stone or the sheikh. What heals them is the power of their own brains: The Placebo Effect.

One of medicine's greatest mysteries is this: If a patient truly believes that the sugar pill they swallow is a miraculous medicine, the brain opens its own pharmacy and secretes the chemicals to heal the body. Alchemists market this biological mechanism as their own miracle.

The metaphor that best explains this is Disney's famous movie *Dumbo*. The flying elephant Dumbo doesn't believe he can fly. His friend gives him a crow's feather and says, "This is a magic feather, if you hold this, you will fly." Dumbo holds the feather and flies. At the end of the movie, he drops the feather but continues to fly. At that moment, he realizes that the skill was not in the feather, but in himself.

Modern Alchemists (Charlatans, Energy Experts) sell us that "Magic Feather" at an exorbitant price. What cures our headache is not the quantum device, but our belief. The Alchemist sells our power back to us as their own miracle.

The Sunk Cost Fallacy: Why Can't We Wake Up?

The final and most painful question: Why don't people run away when they realize they've been scammed? Why do they continue to defend fake prophets? The answer to this is hidden in the economic concept of the "Sunk Cost Fallacy."

If you have invested too much effort, time, money, and reputation into a path, it becomes impossible to accept that the path is wrong. Imagine a person who has given 20 years of their life to a cult. All their friends are there, all their past is there, all their identity is there. Can they wake up one morning and say, "It turns out our sheikh was a scammer, I threw 20 years of my life in the trash"? This confession means the suicide of the ego.

Therefore, even if the facts (scandals, thefts, lies) are exposed; disciples defend their leaders with even greater fanaticism. "This is a test," they say. "Our sheikh knows something we don't," they say. Because accepting that you have been played for a fool is more painful than continuing to be deceived.

Alchemists know this very well. That's why they make their victims accomplices. They integrate them into the system so much that breaking away becomes equivalent to dying.

Conclusion: The Alchemist is Within Us

With this additional session, we understand this:

Alchemists are not aliens coming from the outside.

They are parasites that settle into our inner;

- Void of loneliness (Love Bombing),
- Hope for healing (Placebo),
- And ego that is afraid of making mistakes (Sunk Cost).

The way to expel them from the laboratory passes through first recognizing these voids within ourselves.

CONCLUSION: THE SONG OF THE SIRENS AND TYING ONESELF TO THE MAST

In ancient Greek mythology, there is an island that is the nightmare of sailors: The Island of the Sirens. The half-bird, half-woman creatures (Sirens) living on this island sing a song so enchanting that no sailor who hears this voice can resist them. The song appeals to the deepest desires of the human soul. “Come…” they say, “There is no pain here, there is infinite pleasure here, here your dreams come true.” Captains who hear this song turn the helm to the island, sailors jump into the sea, and ships crash against the rocks and shatter. Just like the shattered lives of those who get carried away by the promises of Alchemists, Ponzis, or Cult Leaders.

However, there is only one mortal in history who managed to survive passing this island: Odysseus. Odysseus’s success was not being stronger or having more willpower than the Sirens. His secret was accepting his own weakness. Odysseus knew that the moment he heard that song, he would lose his mind. His intelligence, his logic, his education would be useless. At that moment, he would simply become an animal desiring.

Therefore, before approaching the island, he made a brilliant plan:

- He tightly plugged the ears of his crew with beeswax. (Thus they would not hear the song and would just do their jobs).
- He had himself tied tightly to the mast of the ship with ropes.
- And he gave a strict order to his crew: “No matter how much I beg, do not untie me!”

As the ship passed by the island, Odysseus heard the song. He went crazy. He screamed, he struggled to break free from the ropes, to jump into the sea, to reach that treasure. But the ropes (rules) held him. The crew (system) didn’t hear him. And the ship glided past the disaster. Odysseus survived.

The Masts of the Modern World: Pre-commitment

Today, this strategy of Odysseus is called the “Ulysses Contract,” and in behavioral economics, it is called “Pre-commitment.”

Postmodern Alchemists are everywhere.

- The notification sound on our phone is the song of the Sirens.
- The green candles on the crypto exchange are the song of the Sirens.
- The politician or sheikh saying "I will give you heaven" is the song of the Sirens.

Saying "I will resist this sound with my willpower" is the mistake Newton made. Willpower is a depleting resource. If you hear that song when you are tired in the evening, when you are lonely, or when you are in debt, you will jump into the sea.

The only way to salvation is to tie yourself to the mast.

What are these masts?

- **Financial Masts:** These are savings instructions where money automatically goes to a private pension system (BES) or gold on payday, which are hard to cash out. (Prevents impulsive spending).
- **Mental Masts:** These are pre-written, inflexible rules such as "I don't enter a business I don't know," "I don't invest with debt," "If someone promises me very high profits, I leave the table."
- **Social Masts (Beeswax):** Unfollowing accounts that create FOMO, muting WhatsApp groups that say "We are flying, we are taking off." It is cutting out the noise

True Alchemy: The Triumph of the Boring

Let's return to the beginning of the book, to that dark basement where Hennig Brand boiled urine.

Alchemists searched for the "Shortcut" for centuries. They wanted to turn lead (the worthless) into gold (the valuable) in an instant. An effortless, timeless, painless transformation...

But the universe has an immutable law:

Everything valuable is formed with time and effort.

- True wealth; is formed not with a lottery ticket, but with years of disciplined saving and compound interest.
- True knowledge; is formed not with a weekend course, but with thousands of pages of reading and experience.
- True reputation; is built not with an Instagram filter, but with years of honesty.

The biggest lie Postmodern Alchemists sell us is the lie that life can be accelerated. Whereas if 9 months are needed for a baby to be born, time is also needed for a fortune or a character to be born.

True Alchemy is patience.

True Alchemy is effort.

True Alchemy is being able to say "I will hoe my garden" while everyone else is chasing after a "Magic Wand."

Final Word: The Captain's Cabin

You have read this book. You entered the alchemists' laboratory, saw their tricks, and understood the psychology of the victims (and ourselves).

Now when you hear that song, you will know that it is not an opportunity, but a trap.

Now all you have to do is tie yourself tightly to the mast of your own ship and plug your ears to those sweet lies.

Remember:

That "Secret Formula" that will make you rich, save you, make you happy is not outside, in someone else's hands.

That formula is hidden in your effort, your mind, and your patience.

The Sirens will continue to sing.

But you know your course now.

Welcome home!

CONCEPT INVENTORY

INTRODUCTION & CHAPTER 1

Alchemy:

Historically, the art of turning worthless metals into gold, curing diseases, and finding the elixir of immortality. In our book, however; it is used as the "illusion" of turning a worthless asset (empty promise) into an invaluable opportunity in people's eyes.

Philosopher's Stone (Lapis Philosophorum):

The legendary substance alchemists tried to attain. It is believed to turn the metal it touches into gold and grant immortality to its owner. Its equivalent in the modern world is; the formula for "getting rich quick."

Use Value vs. Exchange Value:

The difference between what a good is useful for (Use Value) and how much it is sold for in the market (Exchange Value). The Alchemist is the person who markets something with a use value of "zero" (for example, a digital token) in a way that its exchange value becomes "millions.".

CHAPTER 2

Intelligence Paradox (The Intelligence Trap):

The situation where smart and educated people fail to notice simple frauds due to overconfidence in their own minds. Because intelligence feeds arrogance, it can sometimes be a blinding factor rather than a protective one. (See: Isaac Newton).

Puffers:

The name given to fake alchemists because of the "Puff, puff" sound they made while stoking the alchemy furnaces in the Middle Ages. Today; they are the ancestors of the speculators who pump "empty air" in the stock market, crypto market, or social media.

Illusion of Complexity (Complexity Bias):

People's tendency to believe that things that look complex are more true or valuable. Scammers use this vulnerability by hiding their simple lies with technical terms, charts, and fancy words.

CHAPTER 3

The Greater Fool Theory:

The increase in the price of an asset, independent of its true value, solely with the expectation that "another fool will be found to buy it for more." The person at the end of the chain becomes the "Greatest Fool" and pays the whole bill.

FOMO (Fear of Missing Out):

The fear of missing out on an opportunity. It is the main fuel of herd psychology. It is the situation where an individual who sees others winning abandons rational thought and invests in panic.

Nigredo (Black Phase):

In alchemy, the first stage where matter rots and blackens. In financial markets, however; it represents the moment of collapse when the bubble bursts, panic begins, and dreams of wealth turn into steam.

CHAPTER 4

Post-Truth:

The situation where objective facts become less important than emotions and personal beliefs in shaping public opinion. It is the mentality of "It doesn't matter if it's true or not, does it make me feel good?".

Fake It Till You Make It:

The strategy of acting like someone you are not (rich, successful, happy), convincing people of it, and eventually actually reaching that position. It is the fundamental motto of Anna Delvey and Influencer culture.

Snapchat Dysmorphia:

The psychology of a person looking at their filtered and digitally corrected photo and not liking, or even hating, their real face in the mirror.

Simulacra:

French philosopher Jean Baudrillard's concept. A "copy/image" that replaces reality and looks more real than reality itself. (E.g.: The Instagram photo of a vacation giving more satisfaction than the vacation itself).

CHAPTER 5

Spiritual Materialism:

The disease of using spirituality (yoga, meditation, religion) not to file down the ego, but to polish the ego even more, gain status, and feel like a chosen person.

Placebo Effect:

The biological healing response a person gives to an ineffective substance (sugar pill, charlatan's prayer, energy stone) because they believe it will work. The power of the brain to heal by tricking itself.

Sunk Cost Fallacy:

The inability to abandon a job or belief because too much effort/money has been spent on it, even when it is understood to be wrong. It is the inability to say "Cutting your losses is a profit," and sinking even deeper to avoid accepting the loss.

Love Bombing:

The tactic of cults or manipulative leaders to make a newcomer emotionally dependent by showering them with excessive attention, love, and praise.

CONCLUSION

Pre-commitment:

A person anticipating the moments when their willpower will weaken and setting binding rules for themselves in advance. (Odysseus having himself tied to the mast).

Ulysses Contract:

A binding agreement a person makes with their present mind to prevent their future self from making mistakes. (E.g.: Setting up an automatic savings instruction).

BIBLIOGRAPHY AND INSPIRING WORKS

Books

- **Baudrillard, Jean.** *Simulacra and Simulation.* (University of Michigan Press).
- **Chancellor, Edward.** *Devil Take the Hindmost: A History of Financial Speculation.* (Plume / Penguin Random House).
- **Coelho, Paulo.** *The Alchemist.* (Harper Collins).
- **De Botton, Alain.** *Status Anxiety.* (Pantheon / Penguin Random House).
- **Debord, Guy.** *The Society of the Spectacle.* (Zone Books).
- **Ehrenreich, Barbara.** B*right-sided: How the Relentless Promotion of Positive Thinking Has Undermined America.* (Metropolitan Books).
- **Eliade, Mircea.** *The Forge and the Crucible: The Origins and Structures of Alchemy.* (Univ. of Chicago Press).

- **Fromm, Erich.** *Escape from Freedom.* (Farrar, Straus and Giroux).
- **Kindleberger, Charles P.** *Manias, Panics, and Crashes: A History of Financial Crises.* (Palgrave Macmillan).
- **Mackay, Charles.** *Extraordinary Popular Delusions and the Madness of Crowds.* (Wordsworth Editions).
- **McIntyre, Lee.** *Post-Truth.* (MIT Press).
- **Robson, David.** *The Intelligence Trap: Why Smart People Make Dumb Mistakes.* (W. W. Norton & Company).
- **Sagan, Carl.** *The Demon-Haunted World: Science as a Candle in the Dark.* (Ballantine Books).
- **Shiller, Robert J.** *Irrational Exuberance.* (Princeton University Press).
- **Storr, Anthony.** *Feet of Clay: Saints, Sinners, and Madmen: A Study of Gurus.* (Free Press / Simon & Schuster).
- **Taleb, Nassim Nicholas.** *The Black Swan: The Impact of the Highly Improbable.* (Random House).
- **Trungpa, Chögyam.** *Cutting Through Spiritual Materialism.* (Shambhala Publications).
- **White, Michael.** *Isaac* Newton: *The Last Sorcerer.* (Fourth Estate / HarperCollins).
- **Williams, Rachel DeLoache.** *My Friend Anna: The True Story of a Fake Heiress.* (Gallery Books / Simon & Schuster).

- **Zuckoff, Mitchell.** *Ponzi's Scheme: The True Story of a Financial Legend.* (Random House).

Articles and Research

- **MIT Media Lab.** Vosoughi, S., Roy, D., & Aral, S. (2018). "The spread of true and false news online." *Science,* 359(6380), 1146-1151.
- **Boston Post Archives. (1920).** Original investigative reports on Charles Ponzi and International Reply Coupons.

NOTES

NOTES

www.ingramcontent.com/pod-product-compliance
Lightning Source LLC
Chambersburg PA
CBHW071354230926
51846CB00002B/552
9786255765291